UNDERSTANDING
Vincent
VAN GOGH

Frederick Dawe

An analysis of the paintings and drawings of one of
the most violent creative spirits of the 19th century

*Self-portrait in front of the
Easel*
1888
Oil on canvas
$25\frac{1}{2} \times 20$ in
(65 × 50.5 cm)
Rijksmuseum
Vincent Van Gogh,
Amsterdam

Published by A&W
VISUAL LIBRARY
New York and London
Originated, designed and
produced by Trewin
Copplestone Publishing
Ltd, London
© Trewin Copplestone
Publishing Ltd 1976

Filmset and
reproduced by
Photoprint Plates Ltd,
Rayleigh, Essex
Printed in Great Britain by
Chromoworks Ltd,
Nottingham

Library of Congress
Catalog Card Number:
75-37498
ISBN 0-89104-036-6

Van Gogh: His Life and Times

Vincent Van Gogh did not become a painter until he reached the age of twenty-eight, and it was only in the last three years of his life, racked by insanity and loneliness, that he flowered into genius and produced the greater part of the paintings and drawings for which he is now famous.

He was born on 30th March, 1853, in Groot Zundert, in the Dutch province of North Brabant, the eldest son of a Protestant minister. His first employment was as a gallery salesman in the Hague branch of his uncle's firm, the art dealers, Goupil. In 1873 the firm transferred him to their London branch, where he promptly fell in love with his landlady's daughter. In 1875 he was again transferred, this time to the firm's headquarters in Paris. But a year later he was dismissed for being moody and irritable with the customers.

Two months after this dismissal, Van Gogh returned to England, and began teaching elementary French in a small school in Ramsgate. He soon began to consider the possibility of becoming a lay preacher, a career which would give expression to his powerful mystical bent, and he went home to think about his future. He took a job in a bookshop in Dordrecht, but after a few months moved to Amsterdam, where he prepared to take entrance examinations for university, in order to study theology. Concerned by the difference between the teachings in the Bible and the actual practices of the Church, Van Gogh went instead to Brussels to train as a missionary. In 1878, he volunteered to go to the Belgian mining district of the Borinage as an evangelical preacher, and into this work he threw himself totally.

Portrait of the Artist's Mother
1888
Oil on canvas
15½ × 12¼ in
(39.4 × 33.7 cm)
Norton Simon Foundation,
Los Angeles

View from Van Gogh's Room in the rue Lépic
1887
Pencil and pen, washed
15½ × 21 in
(39.5 × 53.5 cm)
Rijksmuseum
Vincent Van Gogh,
Amsterdam

Portrait of the Artist's Father 1881 Pencil and chinese ink with white gouache 13 × 9¾ in (33 × 22 cm)
Collection Mrs A. R. W. Nieuwenhuizen, Segaar-Aarse, The Hague

Ox Wagon in the Snow
(from a series of Four
Seasons)
1884
Pen and ink
2 × 5¼ in
(5 × 13.5 cm)
R. W. van Hoey Smith
Collection,
Rockanje, Netherlands

The Potato Diggers (from a
series of Four Seasons)
1884
Pen and ink
2 × 5 in
(5 × 13 cm)
R. W. van Hoey Smith
Collection,
Rockanje, Netherlands

His devotion to the miners, and the great support that he gave them during their difficult strikes and in their poverty, led to his being dismissed by the mission. But he continued to live in the district for a while in abject poverty and great spiritual despair, and it was during this period that he first started to draw.

Encouraged by his younger brother, Theo, who was by this time working for Goupil, and who could afford to send him a small allowance, Van Gogh took lessons in drawing and painting in Brussels and made the decision to become a painter. His early pictures are clumsy and heavy, both in line and colour, expressive of his melancholy and depression. He worked under several influences, notably that of the French painter of peasants, Jean-François Millet (1814-75), but he also copied many pictures in different museums and galleries. By 1885, when his father died, he was painting more under the influence of the style of Rubens, and the work of the Japanese print makers, both of which began to make him aware of the emotional value of brighter colours. In February 1886, he went to Paris to live with his brother, Theo, and there he met some of the Impressionists, including Camille Pissarro (1831-1903), and Edgar Degas (1834-1917), as well as other painters who were there at the time such as Henri de Toulouse-Lautrec (1864-1901), Georges Seurat (1859-91) and Paul Gauguin (1848-1903).

In spite of his brother's efforts, he did not succeed in selling any of his paintings in Paris, and indeed, by the time he died, only one of his pictures had actually been sold. It was in 1885 that the first of his notable pictures, the sombre *Potato Eaters* was painted, but his meeting with the brightly coloured

*Van Gogh's House on the
Place Lamartine, Arles*
(The Yellow House)
1888
Oil on canvas
30 × 37 in
(76 × 94 cm)
Rijksmuseum
Vincent Van Gogh,
Amsterdam

The Painter on the Road to Tarascon
1888
Oil on canvas
19 × 17⅞ in
(48 × 44 cm)
Formerly Kaiser Friedrich Museum,
Magdeburg

palette of the Impressionists put an end to this use of dark colours. In February 1888, he moved to the south of France, to the town of Arles, in search of sun and colour, and it was here that his most intense and productive period began. He hoped to establish in Arles an artists colony, and towards this end his brother Theo rented for him a small house, where later on in the year, Paul Gauguin, the French painter who later rejected Western civilization and went to live in Tahiti, joined him at Theo's request. The two did not manage to live together harmoniously, however, and after a final quarrel, Van Gogh, in a fit, attempted to kill his friend, and then cut off the lobe of his own ear. Gauguin informed Theo, and wisely left. In 1889, Van Gogh was admitted to the hospital of the Saint Paul de Mausole at Saint-Rémy-en-Provence, where he continued to paint in spite of breaks in his sanity. In 1890, he paid two short visits to Theo in Paris, but finally felt impelled to place himself in the medical care of Dr Gachet, a friend of several of the Impressionists. Two months later he shot himself, and died on 29th July, 1890.

As many details of his life indicate, Van Gogh was over-sensitive and fanatically religious at the best of times. At the worst of times he was insane and utterly lonely, his excesses of temperament tending to alienate his friends and family except for his brother

Van Gogh's Bedroom at Arles
1888
Oil on canvas
28⅜ × 35½ in
(72 × 90 cm)
Rijksmuseum
Vincent Van Gogh,
Amsterdam

4

Paul Gauguin: *Portrait
of Van Gogh painting
Sunflowers in Arles*
1888
Oil on canvas
28¾ × 36¼ in
(73 × 92.1 cm)
Rijksmuseum
Vincent Van Gogh,
Amsterdam

Theo, who consistently stood by him. His rejection by women, and by Gauguin, whom he idolized, led to periods of great depression, and moments of real despair. However, during the nine years in which he painted, Van Gogh completed over six hundred canvases and nearly a thousand drawings and water colours, the greater part of the works of real genius being produced during his period at Arles. His greatest paintings are charged with an extraordinary intensity of feeling, and great awareness of truth and nature. His remarkable letters give a passionate survey of the life of this lonely, radical and very human painter, overcharged with an emotional intensity and insight which few people could bear, and which most people, during his short lifetime, completely ignored.

*Japonaiserie: The Bridge
in the Rain* (after Hiroshige)
1887
Oil on canvas
28¾ × 21¼ in
(73 × 54 cm)
Rijksmuseum
Vincent Van Gogh
Amsterdam

Self-portrait
1886
Pencil
8¼ × 7¼ in
(21 × 18 cm)
Rijksmuseum
Vincent Van Gogh,
Amsterdam

Composition

Van Gogh's compositions were usually based on the simplest of line structures. One particularly interesting compositional technique that he used, he learned from the Impressionists.

The artist placed the centre of interest in the topmost part of the picture, and left a large expanse of relatively unfilled space in the lower part: we can see this technique used in *The Enclosed Field* opposite. All the points of interest, such as the house, trees and hills, are placed at the very top of the drawing, leaving the life-filled cornfield in the foreground. Van Gogh used the same

Still-life: Vase with Sunflowers
1888
Oil on canvas
$36\frac{3}{8} \times 28\frac{7}{8}$ in
(92.5×73 cm)
National Gallery.
London

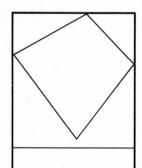

Analytical diagram of *Still-life: Vase with Sunflowers*

compositional device in the canvas *The Drawbridge at Langlois* of 1888 (grey version), in which all the points of interest, including the subject of the painting, are placed in the top quarter of the picture area, wedged in and supported by a relatively uninteresting view of pathways and grassy patches.

A compositional problem which Van Gogh had to deal with constantly was connected with the fact that the dynamic vitality of the forms that he painted tended to escape the limitations of the edge of the canvas. Even when he painted relatively 'flat' forms such as the sky, the sea or a backcloth to a portrait, he treated them in such a way that they took on a dynamic curvilinear movement or a rhythm of their own. To help himself to contain these curves, rhythms and dancing forms within the four straight edges of his canvas, he would sometimes establish a series of straight lines within the series of curves and rounded forms in order that these would then find a harmony with the straight edges of the canvas, and with the final straight edge of the frame.

We look at the vital, glowing *Still-life: Vase with Sunflowers* which he painted to decorate Gauguin's bedroom in Arles for an unexpected example of this. As we mention on page 8, this picture is given a kind of stability and link with the frame through the insistent straight blue lines of the table edge, and is actually based on a composition which contains the excitingly rhythmic sunflower heads in a four-sided structure, which is itself tied into the frame. In this way, Van Gogh eases the round and highly-charged flowers into the rectangle of the canvas, without either the flowers or the straight edge of the picture suffering in any noticeable manner. (See diagram.)

Use of Colour

Van Gogh's use of colour is always aimed at stimulating the emotions. Whenever possible he places in close proximity, colours which in theory clash and which in clashing, set a high emotional tone to the picture. In some cases this clash might be intense, such as in the canvas *The Night Café on the Place Lamartine, Arles* shown on page 28, in which the yellows and oranges of the artificial gas lighting and the floor clash with the reds and greens of the walls and ceiling of the café. Both *The Evening Walk* and the *Still-Life: Vase with Sunflowers* are examples of a more delicate clash which in the still-life is cleverly introduced to set up a subtle resonance of vibration throughout the entire picture. It is painted entirely in different hues of yellows, oranges, and lime greens, all of which are individually exciting, but all of which to a certain extent harmonize with one another. The subtle element of clash, however, which raises the emotional level of the whole painting, is in the delicate blue line which Van Gogh uses to sketch in the edge of the table, the lower section of the base of the vase, and his own short signature, 'Vincent'. We can study the extent to which the vitality of this painting seems to require the thin blue line, by covering up the lower section of the picture and observing the way in which the life

Portrait of Armand Roulin
1888
$25\frac{5}{8} \times 21\frac{3}{4}$ in
(65.1×55.2 cm)
Folkwang Museum,
Essen

and vitality of the sunflowers is diminished in consequence.

A major change in Van Gogh's use of colour came when he moved away from the use of dark, drab and heavy hues, characteristic of his early paintings such as *The Potato Eaters* to the use of somewhat less gloomy colours and stronger impastos as a result of studying Rubens and Japanese prints. But it was when he reached Paris and became familiar with the work of the Impressionists that he learned the use of bright colours. And it was there, that he learned from Gauguin the method of using large areas of pure colour as backgrounds to act as foils for his strong linear rhythms. He was especially fond of contrasting flat areas of blue, whether the Mediterranean sea, the sky, or an 'abstract' background or curtain, with details of yellow or orange.

If Van Gogh wanted to convey a mood of depression, or of the macabre in a portrait, he would silhouette his heads against a contrasting background of blue or green, as in his *Portrait of Armand Roulin*, illustrated here. The great subtlety of these 'flat' backgrounds lies in the fact that they are never really flat, but built from gradations of colour which have a vitality of texture and variety of hue which prevent them from being monotonous. Only a colourist of Van Gogh's capability could get away with such a liberal use of green as a background as in the portrait of Postman Joseph Roulin on page 21. The conflict which the green establishes with the reddish hue of the skin, and with the red of the lips, leads to an expressionist intensity of feeling which might have been merely tasteless in the hands of a lesser master.

9

Drawing Methods

Peasant Digging
1882
Pen and pencil
$19\frac{1}{4} \times 11\frac{1}{4}$ in
(49 × 28.5 cm)
Rijksmuseum
Vincent Van Gogh,
Amsterdam

*Peasant Binding Corn
Sheaves*
1885
Black chalk
$17\frac{1}{2} \times 23$ in
(44.5 × 58.5 cm)
Rijksmuseum
Kröller-Müller,
Otterlo

*Landscape near
Montmajour, with the little
Train from Arles to Oryon*
1888
Reed pen and black chalk
$19\frac{1}{4} \times 24$ in
(49 × 61 cm)
British Museum, London

It must be admitted that many of Van Gogh's early drawings are clumsy and harsh, but we must recognize that he himself frequently claimed that he was not drawing to gain praise or admiration, but to give expression to his feelings about the world. Most of his early drawings, of miners and peasants, are done with very noticeable line contours. We might even say that the line which marks the skirted back of the stooping woman is too hard and tends to destroy the sense of form, or that the line along the left leg of the digging peasant is too heavy, like several of the lines along his clothing. Van Gogh also maintained that the style in which he would draw a peasant could not possibly be the same as the style suitable for drawing a duke or a king, for the artist would want to express different emotions about the two types of people. Of his first really impressive picture, a group of peasants at their frugal evening meal, *The Potato Eaters*, illustrated on page 15, he said, 'I wanted to give the impression of quite a different way of living than that of us civilized people. Therefore I am not at all anxious for everyone to like or to admire it at once'. This feeling pervades his early drawings, and we may infer from these words that he did not seek to make his drawings and paintings graceful or delicate in the accepted sense of the words.

However, as his genius ripened, he did begin to dispense with the heavy line, and he began to see the virtue and expressive quality which textures and broken lines might add to his drawings. Almost all his later drawings depend for their expressiveness upon

The Zouave Milliet
1888
Reed Pen
$12\frac{3}{4} \times 9\frac{1}{2}$ in
(32.5 × 24 cm)
Solomon R. Guggenheim
Museum,
New York,
Thannhauser Collection

texture, rather than upon quality of line. The texture may be formed from the heavy slashes and cross hatchings which he frequently used in his portraits as in *The Zouave Milliet* or the delicate series of dots and scratches by which he expresses the quality of corn or grass in the vast, wind-swept fields and meadowlands of France. It is upon this strength of texture that the quality of these pictures hang.

An explanation of this must surely be related to Van Gogh's growing awareness of the emotional impact that he wished to give in his work. It was easier for him to convey this in a black and white drawing, through the means of textured areas rather than through single lines. Line may be used to de-scribe form, but it is texture which conveys strong emotional qualities. Thus, in some ways Van Gogh is studying the emotional quality of his subjects when he draws in textures. His finest drawings appear to be as impulsively executed as his paintings, but whilst he worked quickly, he also worked carefully, for as he put it himself, very early in his career, 'the great things are not done by impulse, but by a series of small things brought together. And great things are not something accidental, but most certainly *willed*. What is drawing? How does one learn it? It is working through an invisible iron wall that seems to stand between what one *feels* and what one *can do*'–words that might stand as an epitaph to this great spirit.

Technique

A superficial examination of Van Gogh's painting technique might lead one to imagine that he swirled the oil colours on to his canvas in a savage and unrestrained manner, in the heat of the emotions he wanted to express. In fact, his paintings were deliberately and very coolly planned, his compositions carefully worked out, and the main colour areas painted down on to the canvas long before he applied the heavy impastos or slabs of colour.

Van Gogh's use of paint is always emotional. He applied liberal textures of paint (a technique learned partly from the 'pointillist' painter Georges Seurat (1859-91), which involved the application of small dots of colour on to the canvas, and partly from the heavy impasto work of the artist Adolphe Monticelli (1824-86) whom he greatly admired), and as a result achieved highly charged surfaces of paint, which may be partly seen in reproductions, but which should be seen in the original for the full impact to make itself felt. Sometimes the thick slabs and swirls of paint follow the actual contours of the objects painted, as for example in the area around his right eye in the *Self-portrait in a Grey Felt Hat* opposite. Sometimes, however, they are added merely to lend a disturbing or emotional quality to the

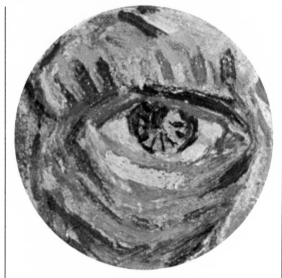

Detail of Van Gogh's right eye from *Self-portrait in a Grey Felt Hat*

surface, such as with the red slabs of colour worked into the blue background around this same head, which have the effect of creating a kind of intense aura around the subject. In this way, Van Gogh adds a quality of spirituality to the form, in much the same way as the haloes of gold added a symbolic spirituality in medieval paintings of saints and holy persons.

As a result of a stay in Antwerp in 1885-6 Van Gogh introduced stronger impastos and somewhat brighter colours into his work, as in the painting *Still-life: Pair of Boots* of 1885, moving away from the very sombre tones of his earlier work. But it was his meeting in Paris with such extreme colourists as Henri de Toulouse-Lautrec (1864-1901) and Gauguin, that caused him to abandon all restraint, and he began painting in the intense yellows, oranges, greens and blues which we now associate with his name. However, we would fail to understand the true quality of Van Gogh's vision and technique if we were to explain his use of colour and paint in terms merely of the influence of the Impressionists. He himself began to see how he differed from them relatively early on, and wrote to his brother Theo, 'I should not be surprised if the Impressionists soon find fault with my way of working, for it has been fertilized by the ideas of Delacroix rather than by theirs. Because, instead of trying to reproduce exactly what I have before my

Still-life: Pair of Boots
c. 1885
On pasteboard
14¾ × 18 in
(36.5 × 45.7 cm)
Rijksmuseum
Vincent Van Gogh,
Amsterdam

eyes, I used colour more arbitrarily so as to express myself more forcefully'. It was not merely through the brighter hues that this expression of emotions was intensified, but by a richer and more luxuriant application of thick impastos and spirals of pigment.

Self-portrait in a Grey Felt Hat 1887 $17\frac{1}{4} \times 14\frac{3}{4}$ in (44×37.5 cm) Rijksmuseum Vincent Van Gogh, Amsterdam

Figure Painting and Drawing

The Reaper
1885
Black chalk
17×21¼ in
(43×54 cm)
Rijksmuseum
Vincent Van Gogh,
Amsterdam

The Potato Eaters
1885
Oil on canvas
32¼×45 in
(82×114 cm)
Rijksmuseum
Vincent Van Gogh,
Amsterdam

'You know, the more I think about it, the more I realize that nothing is more truly artistic than to love people', wrote Van Gogh to Theo, and his many paintings of groups and individuals bear out this belief completely. In a sense, he was not drawing and painting individuals so much as portraying himself.

His earliest drawings show people in action, mowing, reaping, or sitting in chairs, eating and even weeping. But the early pencil drawing of an old man weeping, or the rather clumsy charcoal drawing of a peasant mowing the corn are largely anonymous, and certainly not portraits of individuals. The emphasis is on the peasant type, on the humanity which it depicts. The drawing of the old man of 1882 is correctly proportioned,

Detail from *Noon*
1890
Oil on canvas
28¾ × 35⅞ in
(73 × 91 cm)
Musée du Louvre
Paris

Old Man in Sorrow
1882
Black chalk and pencil
19¾ × 12¼ in
(50 × 31 cm)
Rijksmuseum
Vincent Van Gogh,
Amsterdam

so far as the relationship of the different limbs is concerned, but the later drawing of the peasant mowing of 1885 is strongly out of proportion, for the feet are too heavy, the arms too long. Van Gogh has allowed this distortion to enter into his work because he wanted to convey a feeling which an accurate portrayal of the figure would not have done. In this case, he seeks to give a feeling of the rhythmic movement of the mowing, the monotony of it, and the manner in which heavy labour distorts the human being. The lengthened arms make the man monkey-like, and give us a feeling that he has been rendered less than human by his hard task.

The effect of labour and poverty on the physical body, which Van Gogh saw as an expression of the soul, is often the theme of his early drawings, and the main idea in his first masterpiece, *The Potato Eaters*. The picture shows a poor family sitting down to eat their only food, the potatoes, which they have grown themselves. In this picture it is again the humanity which interests Van Gogh, and he portrays each of the individuals very carefully, indeed, so much care and detail does he work into these faces that they become almost caricatures. Van Gogh clearly felt that he could best express the abasement of their spirit and the constriction and the grinding poverty of their lives, by reducing them from a human state to one which is as far removed from human dignity and beauty as is the world of comic strips. Certainly, from what Van Gogh wrote about this picture, quoted on page 10, he was not intending us to admire it, but we eventually find that its message and compelling imagery begin to grow on us, not because the picture is beautiful, but because it is somehow expressive of a state of human existence.

Wheatfield with Cypresses
1889
Oil on canvas
$28\frac{1}{2} \times 36$ in
(72.5 × 91.5 cm)
National Gallery,
London

16

Portrait Drawing

Portrait of Père Tanguy
1887
Pencil
8½ × 5¼ in
(21 × 13 cm)
Rijksmuseum
Vincent Van Gogh,
Amsterdam

Van Gogh did drawings in very many different media – charcoal, pencil, chalk, crayon, pen and ink, and even with lithographic chalks or ink on to stones – but his most impressive drawings are those done with a heavy reed pen and ink. At the height of his development and technical proficiency, he used the pen almost savagely, and the heavy slashes and scribbles carry with them a feeling of impulsive emotionalism which we also sense in the use of colour in his paintings.

The very impressive study of the postman Roulin on the next page, which was drawn in 1888, as one of a series of portraits of his friend, demonstrates admirably Van Gogh's reluctance to use continuous lines as contours. The only strongly-marked contour lines are those on his left shoulder (as opposed to the right shoulder which has a series of

Portrait of Dr Gachet
1890
Etching
7 × 5¾ in
(17.5 × 14.5 cm)
Cabinet d'Estampes,
Amsterdam

lines which dissolve at the edge, and suggest the rotundity of form, the feeling of space as the shoulder curves into the back), the lines along the lapels and the rather broken lines of the postman's hat. We see how Van Gogh has attempted to pull together the background and the clothing, in order to keep the focal point of interest on the face, by using cross-hatching in both cases. However, there is much variety in the handling, for the emphasis in the background is on the horizontal and vertical patches, the cross-hatching itself being light, whereas the thick texture of the clothing is suggested with heavier more diagonal cross-hatching, which tends to follow the forms of the clothing.

It is in the beard and in the face that his real genius for texture and variety of handling is to be found. The luxuriance of the hair, the heavy eyebrows, the delicate modelling of the eyes, the cross-hatching under the hat, down to the points and dots on the cheek, exhibit a wide versatility. This variety is intended to stir our emotions in much the same way as the contrasts of colour in the paintings do.

Postman Roulin 1888 Pen and ink 12½ × 9½ in
(31.5 × 24 cm) H. R. Hahnloser Collection, Bern

Portrait Painting

La Berceuse: Madame Augustine Roulin
1889
Oil on canvas
36½ × 29¼ in
(93 × 74 cm)
Rijksmuseum
Kröller-Müller,
Otterlo

Self-portrait 1889 Oil on canvas
22½ × 17¼ in (57 × 43.5 cm)
John Hay Whitney Collection, New York

Portrait of Dr Gachet 1890 Oil on canvas
26 × 22½ in (66 × 57 cm)
Musée du Louvre, Paris

During the next year, 1889, Van Gogh painted a portrait of his postman friend Roulin–the one person in Arles who had stuck by him during his illness, when the majority of the other townsfolk had drawn up a petition asking for the difficult and eccentric painter to be removed. In this portrait he presents his friend, 'a good soul and so wise and so full of feeling and so trustful', in a masterpiece of composition, against a background of green which is enlivened with an embroidery of flowers.

These flowers serve a dual purpose. First of all, they set up a vibration around the head of Roulin, recalling Van Gogh's own words, 'I would like to paint men or women with the suggestion of the eternal which used to be symbolized by the halo'. Van Gogh is fond of establishing this kind of spiritual

Portrait of Postman Joseph Roulin
1889
Oil on canvas
$25\frac{1}{2} \times 21\frac{1}{4}$ in
(65×54 cm)
Rijksmuseum
Kröller-Müller,
Otterlo

background to his portraits as we saw in his *Self-portrait in a Grey Felt Hat* on page 12, and the vitality of these flowers starts up a dance, especially in the contrast that the red poppy offers to the green, which suggests just such a halo or aura around the head.

The second function of the circular flower forms is to establish a link between the background and the portrait head itself. The series of over twenty round blobs of flower heads on the background is echoed in a series of round shapes on Roulin himself. His two buttons are round, although, in fact, the one on the left is also spiral-formed, because of the way in which Van Gogh has brushed in the impasto of yellow over the orange, to suggest its shining metal surface. It is more like a flower than a button. Another round shape is to be found in the yellow-pink

flesh which appears above the collar below the bearded chin. The beard itself is carefully painted to give emphasis to the curves and spirals of the locks, thereby showing a relationship between the mass of hair and the round forms of the background. The red of the lips might almost be the red of the poppies, and even the form of the hat has been painted so as to emphasize its roundness, rather than in the manner in which it is drawn in the pen portrait on page 19. It is this concern for the way in which the background and subject must be related, and this understanding of the emotional quality of the use of circles and spirals, which accounts for the way in which Van Gogh may paint the portrait of an ordinary postman, and yet somehow construct, thereby, a masterpiece of composition and design.

21

Landscape Drawing

Detail from *Path through a Field with Willows*

Path through a Field with Willows
1888
Pen and ink
$10 \times 13\frac{3}{4}$ in
(25.4 × 34 cm)
Rijksmuseum
Vincent Van Gogh,
Amsterdam

The lovely pen and ink drawing of 1888, *Path through a Field with Willows* makes an interesting comparison with the study of a *Street in Auvers* (La Maison du Père Pilon) of 1890, made in pencil and violet ink. In this comparison, we can observe several important developments. In the earlier drawings straight lines are used only where it is absolutely necessary, as for example in the vine railings, in the walls of the house and in the trees. All the other parts of the drawing are done in textures, and the contours of the forms are dissolved in a surface tension of flecks of ink, cross-hatching and dots.

In the street scene at Auvers, however, Van Gogh has tended to pull his forms into rounded shapes – this is especially notice-

Street in Auvers
(La Maison du Père Pilon)
1890
Charcoal, pen and violet ink
17½ × 21¾ in
(44.5 × 55 cm)
Rijksmuseum
Vincent Van Gogh,
Amsterdam

able in the handling of the grass around the footpaths, and even in the foliage of the trees. In this later drawing the emotional impact does not come only from the texture of the line, but also from the curvilinear forms into which the textures have been marshalled.

No doubt this emotional charge has been injected into the view of Auvers because of Van Gogh's own intense state of mind, for it was executed in the last year of his life, when he was in one of the short rest periods during his insanity. The handling of the trees and grass reminds us of the painting, *Cypresses with Two Figures* illustrated on page 25, which he also executed in the last year of his life. In it, the emphasis on the construction of the curvilinear forms of the trees, conveys their strong emotional impact on the sensitivity of the artist. These rapid flicks of texture, bound up in the curious curves, take us a few years beyond Van Gogh and point to the important influence that he was to have on the work of the Norwegian Expressionist Edvard Munch (1863-1944). Perhaps, had Van Gogh not died so tragically,

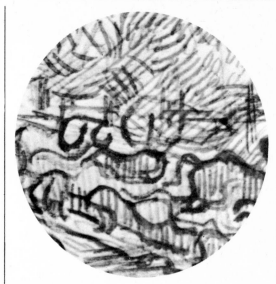

Detail from *Street in Auvers*

he would have continued in the direction hinted at in these later works, and have developed an Expressionist style. Like the work of Munch, it might have become more abstract and, at the same time, an even more powerful expression of his emotions.

Landscape Painting

The Langlois Bridge with
Women washing
1888
Oil on canvas
$21\frac{1}{4} \times 25\frac{1}{2}$ in
(54×65 cm)
Rijksmuseum
Kröller-Müller,
Otterlo

In *Cypresses with Two
Figures* the moon is
wrongly lit by the sun

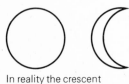

In reality the crescent
should arch towards the
source of light as above

Van Gogh's *Cypresses with Two Figures* was painted only two months before his suicide, and it is a highly-charged landscape which utilizes all the painterly devices for which he is now famous. In both this painting and in *The Langlois Bridge*, the colour is based on a strong clash between the oranges and yellows and the blues of the sky and water. The conflict and dissonance between them sets the main 'tone' or feeling in both these pictures. In the *Cypresses with Two Figures* neither the yellow nor the blue area is pure in colour, but is textured with impastos and variations of hue which express the tortured mind of the painter, and convey a sense of his impassioned unrest to the spectator. The corn will not stay still–it has been laid down on the canvas with slabs of yellow impasto, all placed in different directions, as though caught in some terrific wind. The sky is also restless, with white fleck-impasto clouds, and with a white aura around the sun, a yel-

low aura around the crescent moon.

The cypress trees, wedged between the sun and moon, are tortured growths of writhing green impastos, casting with the corn a strong *green* shadow, which is thrown not, as we might expect, from the light of the sun but from the light of the moon. By a device such as this, Van Gogh excites a sense of unreality and disquiet in the mind of the spectator–feelings similar to those created by the Italian surrealist painter, Giorgio de Chirico (b. 1888) a few years later. To add visual disquiet, Van Gogh fails to paint in the shadow from the horse and carriage to the right of the composition, so that there is something unreal and ghostly about its substance. A brilliant sun, and a brilliant though impossibly orientated lunar crescent, add to our confusion and intensify the sense of insanity within the structure of the picture. Perhaps within this image we may sense something of Van Gogh's own confusion even in lucid moments, and see another meaning to his words, 'I always feel I am a traveller, going somewhere to some other destination'. Perhaps the two travellers standing at the bottom of the canvas repre-sent Van Gogh and the *alter ego* of his inner conflict, from which his insanity arose.

Cypresses with Two Figures 1889 Oil on canvas
36½ × 29¾ in (92 × 73 cm)
Rijksmuseum Kröller-Müller, Otterlo

Still-life Painting

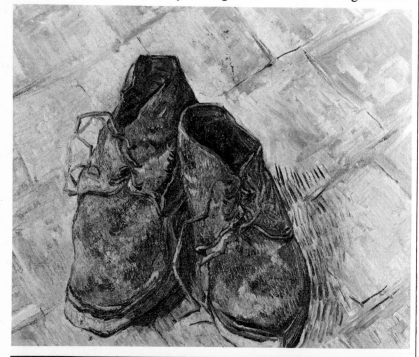

Like most artists when they are first learning to paint, Van Gogh found the drawing and painting of still-life subjects invaluable as an aid to development. Still-lifes, unlike people and even to some extent unlike landscapes, will keep still, and thus allow the artist to study at length the external arrangement of shape, form and colour, and at the same time to investigate the effect of these arranged objects on the inner world of his emotional response. However, Van Gogh's mystical strain was far too strong for him to produce pictures which were simply straightforward portrayals of objects—for him the objects that he portrayed had somehow to be symbolic. If he painted or drew a pair of old shoes, they stood not so much as a pair of shoes, but more as symbols of all the labour and sacrifice of the individual who had worn them: they were fragments of humanity, more than fragments of leather.

Again, in his *Still-life with a Bible* of 1885, we see at least two levels of symbolism. The candlestick represents human emotions, and their concept of truth, which might be lit up by the Bible, a source of spiritual light in this dark world, for those 'with eyes to see'. The only strong colour in this otherwise almost monochromatic picture is the flimsy yellow paper-back book in front of the Bible, which is the other object of Van Gogh's symbolism. This time it is an aspect of humanity, for the book is the novel *La Joie de Vivre* (The Joy of Living) by the great French writer, Emile Zola, whom Van Gogh admired for the clarity and strength of his realistic novels, in which he found 'something solid and strong that can give us strength in the days when we feel weak'.

As Van Gogh's genius began to emerge, these solid and heavy symbolic moralities eventually gave place to light, vital and highly-coloured symbols—flowers and sunflowers, yellow chairs and rocking chairs which became the chief subjects for his still-life paintings, all with their own inner story to tell if one is prepared to listen.

For here is a truth more important to the work of Van Gogh than to most other artists: we must listen with our emotions to these pictures if we are to grasp their inner meaning. It must be careful listening for the initial impact and shock of the images readily stirs our emotions, and we may easily be captured by the sheer delight of colour, texture and imagery, without seeking to ex-

The Artist's Chair 1888-9 Oil on canvas
36¾×28⅞ in (92.5×73 cm) Tate Gallery, London

Still-life with Clogs
1884-5
Oil on canvas
15⅝×16⅜ in
(39×41.5 cm)
Rijksmuseum
Kröller-Müller,
Otterlo

plore deeper below this emotional surface, and hear that quiet, though insistent voice, telling us the nature of reality which underlies the emotional life of man. If we fail to listen deeply, the *The Artist's Chair* is merely a picture of a yellow chair, and his *Sunflowers* remains merely a picture of a few sunflowers.

If we look at two such paintings with real attention, we may find it difficult to say which of the two subjects is more alive. Naturally, the contours and forms of the flowers tend to lend themselves more easily to his vitality of handling which conveys their radiant splendour, but somehow, by the sheer magic of his brush, Van Gogh so infuses life into the yellow wood of the chair that he manages to convey a vitality almost as convincing as that of the flowers. We feel that the chair takes on the appearance of a restless animal, ready to move across the tiled floor at any moment. The magic of this chair is such that even as we look at it, and see in it the hints of all those people who have sat on it, and who will sit on it in the future, we may dimly realise that from the depths of his lonely and troubled soul, this great artist is saying that there is nothing which is ordinary, nothing which is not alive and which does not possess a soul.

Sunflowers
c. 1887
Oil on canvas
23½×39¼ in
(59.5×99.5 cm)
Rijksmuseum
Kröller-Müller,
Otterlo

Picture Analysis:
The Café Terrace
The Night Café

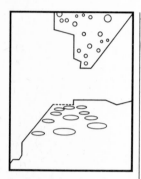

Analytical drawing of
*The Café Terrace on the
Place du Forum, Arles,
at Night*

*The Night Café on the
Place Lamartine, Arles*
1888
Oil on canvas
27½ × 35 in
(70 × 89 cm)
Yale University Art Gallery,
New Haven,
Bequest of Stephen
Carlton Clark

Van Gogh painted the powerful picture of *The Café Terrace on the Place du Forum, Arles, at Night* at the height of his short artistic career, only two years before his death. On a superficial examination the picture appears to be merely a café scene at night, in which Van Gogh contrasts the glare of the gas-lights with the soft light of the eternal stars. However, a closer examination will show that the composition is intended as a study of the intense loneliness and personal isolation which Van Gogh was experiencing at that time. This was also his theme in *The Night Cafe on the Place Lamartine, Arles,* which was painted in the same month, September, 1888, as *The Café Terrace*. Of them Van Gogh said, 'The problem of painting night scenes and effects upon the spot and actually by night interests me', and it is worth noting the similarities between the intentions behind the two paintings, and the differences in the two realizations.

In both paintings Van Gogh expresses the sense of isolation by placing human beings within his composition in the middle distance, so that while we are aware of their presence, we do not actually see their individual faces. Thus we become more aware of the space between us and them, emphasized by the empty tables, than of any human contact. Those humans who are identifiable, such as the patron in *The Night Café* and the waiter in *The Café Terrace*, are simply cyphers of paint impasto, whilst the figures in the right of *The Café Terrace*, walking along the road, merge into the darkness of the gathering dusk.

In *The Café Terrace* it is a brilliant compositional device which reinforces this sense of isolation and which seems to separate us still further from human contact. Van Gogh has established across the central part of his picture area a slab of interwoven squares and linear forms. (See diagram.) These separate the circular shapes of the stars – which glow with a peculiar intensity as yellow swirls of paint in the deep blue twilight – from the yellowish circles of tables outside the café. The uppermost circles symbolize light from heaven, which Van Gogh in particular yearned to reach. The yellow tables, lit by the man-made yellow light of the gas lamps, are symbols of human loneliness. These two extremes of the stars and the tables are set off by the recurrent interplay of squares and rectangles from which the compositional structure of the picture is built.

The large area of yellow gas light to the left is hardly balanced by the small area of yellow to the right, and the composition is off-balance. Furthermore, the artificial lights of the café are intensified by the clash of the blue of the door jamb, the blue sky, and the greens of the trees. Blues and yellows contrast strongly, and in so doing set up a feeling of conflict between the loneliness of the blue and the warmth of human companionship of the yellows and oranges; yet both remain at a distance from the spectator. The clash of colours in *The Night Café*, however, is much stronger and harsher. The reds and greens convey a much more intense feeling of loneliness. About it Van Gogh wrote in one of his letters to Theo, 'I have tried to express the terrible passions of humanity by means of red and green,' and again in his next letter 'the Café is a place where one can ruin one's self, run mad, or commit a crime. So I have tried to express as it were the powers of darkness in a low drink shop, by soft Louis XV green and malachite, contrasting with yellow green and hard blue

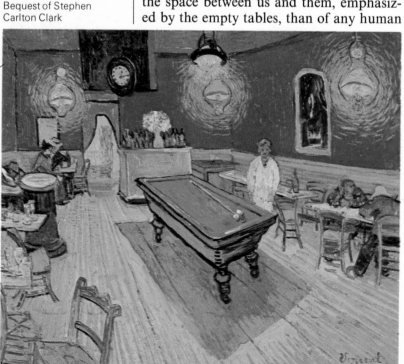

greens, and all this in an atmosphere like a devil's furnace, of pale sulphur'.

It is typical of Van Gogh's expressionist approach that in both these pictures he should seek to underline the sense of alienation established within the subject-matter

The Café Terrace on the Place du Forum. Arles, at Night
1888 Oil on canvas 32 × 25¾ in (81 × 64.5 cm)
Rijksmuseum Kröller-Müller, Otterlo

and the composition by a conflict amongst the colours themselves.

Biographical Outline

1853
March 30: Vincent Van Gogh born to clergyman, Theodorus Van Gogh and his wife, Anna, at Groot Zundert, North Brabant, in Holland.

1857
His brother Theo is born.

1864-8
Educated at an institute in Zevenbergen.

1869
Apprenticed to the firm of Goupil and Company, his uncle's firm of art dealers in the Hague.

1873-4
Moved to Goupil's London branch.
Unhappy love affair with his landlord's daughter caused withdrawal from social contact, and development of a profound religious enthusiasm.
Became discontented with art dealing.

1875
Transferred to Paris to the head office of Goupil, where his discontent grew.

1876
March: Dismissed by Goupil.
April: Returned to England to take up teaching post at Mr Stokes's school in Ramsgate.
July: Moved to London to work with Congregational Minister, Mr Jones in his parish and school.
December: Returned home to Etten to consider his future.

1877
Worked in a bookshop in Dordrecht.
May: Moved to Amsterdam to prepare for entrance examinations to study theology at Amsterdam University. Abandoned this plan.

1878
Entered instead an evangelical training school in Brussels.
November: Volunteered to work in the poor mining district of the Borinage, South Belgium, as a preacher and school teacher

1879
Dismissed by the Brussels mission, who disapproved of his active sympathy towards the miners and his disagreement with the policies of the church.
Stayed in the Borinage district after his dismissal, where he drew the miners and peasants, and became more and more committed to art.

1880
Studied perspective and anatomy in Brussels.
Received from now on an allowance from his brother, Theo, who was working for Goupil in Paris.
Van Gogh's correspondence with Theo and his sister, Willimien, is already copious.

1881
Returned home to his parents to enter into another unhappy love affair, this time with his recently widowed cousin, Kee Vos, and yet more discussions over his intended career.
December: Went to the Hague to work on oil paintings with his cousin, Anton Mauve (1838-88), and mixed with other painters of the Hague School.

1882
Prostitute Sien Hoornik and her child moved into Van Gogh's rooms, a move strongly disapproved of by all his friends and family.

1883
Moved to Drenthe to escape Sien, ending the only significant relationship he was to have with a woman.
December: Went home to his parents, to Neunen, his father's new parish.

1884
Nursed his mother through a serious illness.
Inspired by Eugène Delacroix's (1798-1863) art theories and Emile Zola's writing, Van Gogh was becoming a painter of great strength, but was considered strange and eccentric.

1885
March: Death of his father.
May: Rented his own studio in Neunen.
November: Moved to Antwerp, never again to return to Holland.
Painted *The Potato Eaters*.

1886
January: Attended Antwerp Academy for a short while.
February: Unexpectedly left for Paris to stay with Theo, where he met Impressionist painters, as well as Paul Gauguin (1848-1903) and Henri de Toulouse-Lautrec (1864-1901).
June: Moved to a large flat in Montmartre with Theo.

1887
Organized exhibitions of the work of Louis Anquetin (1861-1932), Emile Bernard (1868-1941), and himself, and of Japanese prints.
Painted the *Portrait of Père Tanguy*.

1888
February: Left for Arles, Provence, to set up an artists community there.
October: Gauguin joined him at Theo's request. The visit ended after Van Gogh's attempt on Gauguin's life, and the cutting of his own right earlobe. Gauguin returned to Paris

Peasants Seated at a Table
1889-90
Charcoal
9½ × 9¾ in
(24 × 25.5 cm)
Rijksmuseum
Vincent Van Gogh, Amsterdam

with Theo, who had been called to Arles, and Van Gogh went into hospital.
Painted *The Sower*, *The Café Terrace on the Place du Forum, Arles, at Night*, and *L'Arlésienne* amongst many other paintings.

1889
Returned briefly to his studio at the Yellow House in Arles, but spent further periods in hospital there, and then at the mental hospital of Saint-Rémy, on account of his frequent mental crises.
April: Theo married Johanna Van Bonger.
Painted amongst many others the *Portrait of Joseph Roulin* (several versions), *Self-portrait with a Bandaged Ear*, and *The Starry Night*.

1890
January: Birth of Theo and Johanna's son, Vincent Willem.
May: Travelled to Paris to stay with Theo. Continued to Auvers-sur-Oise, where he placed himself under the medical supervision of Dr Gachet, a friend of many Impressionist painters. He worked feverishly, but became increasingly unbalanced and depressed.
Painted *Cypresses with Two Figures* and *Portrait of Dr Gachet* during this year.
July 29: Van Gogh died, having shot himself two days previously.

1891
Death of Theo.

The Fountain in the Garden of St Paul's Hospital 1889
Black chalk, reed pen, and brown ink ·
$19\frac{1}{2} \times 18$ in (49.5×46 cm)
Rijksmuseum Vincent Van Gogh, Amsterdam

Location of Major Works

Museum's galleries and collections in North America, and in the rest of the world where examples of Vincent Van Gogh's work can be seen.

Baltimore
Museum of Art

Boston
Museum of Fine Arts

Cambridge
Fogg Art Museum, Harvard University

Chicago
Art Institute

Los Angeles
Norton Simon Foundation

Merion
Barnes Foundation

New Haven
Yale University Art Gallery

New York
Brooklyn Museum;
Kramarsky Trust Fund;
Metropolitan Museum of Art;
Museum of Modern Art;
Thannhauser Foundation;
Whitney Collection

St Louis
St Louis Art Museum

Washington D.C.
National Gallery of Art

Williamstown
Sterling and Francine Clark Institute

Amsterdam
Rijksmuseum
Vincent Van Gogh

Edinburgh
National Gallery of Scotland

Essen
Kunstmuseum

Leningrad
The Hermitage

London
British Museum;
Courtauld Institute Galleries;
Tate Gallery

Moscow
Pushkin Museum

Munich
Neue Pinakothek

Otterlo
Rijksmuseum Kröller-Müller

Paris
Musée du Louvre
Musée Rodin

Rome
Galleria Nazionale d'Arte Moderna

Rotterdam
Museum Boymans-van Beuningen

Sao Paulo
Museu de Arte

Acknowledgements

The Publishers would like to thank all the museums, galleries and owners of private collections for permission to reproduce works in their care or possession. The caption to each illustration gives the location of the subject.

The photographs were provided by the following Cooper-Bridgeman Library, London 16; Hamlyn Group Picture Library, London 2t, br, 3t, c, 7t, 10tl, tr, b, 11, 14t, 18t, b, 26t, 28, 30, 31, 32; Mansell Collection, London 4t, 19, 23b; National Gallery, London 6, 8tl; Photographie Giraudon, Paris 8b, 15t, 20b, 27tl; Rijksmuseum Kröller-Müller, Otterlo 8tr, 20tl, 21, 24, 27b, 29; Stedelijk Museum, Amsterdam 1, 2bl, 3b, 4b, 5t, bl, br, 7b, 12b, 13, 15b, 22, 23t, 26b; Tate Gallery, London 27tr; Trewin Copplestone Publishing, London 14b, 25, Whitney Collection, New York 20tr.

Portrait of Père Tanguy 1887 Oil on canvas 36¼ × 29½ in (92 × 75 cm) Musée Rodin, Paris